5 THINGS A

LEAD EFFECTIVELY

PHIL STEVENSON

wesleyan
publishing
house

Indianapolis, Indiana

CONTENTS

INTRODUCTION

Many lay people are hesitant to commit to leadership in the local church. Often this hesitancy is the result of feeling unprepared. In most education and employment situations, promotion is based upon a certain level of training being successfully completed. However, in ministry, it may be assumed that those asked to lead will automatically know what to do, or that spiritual gifts and a willingness to serve will be all that they need. They are desperate for resources that will give them a sense of competence and preparedness for their new ministry role.

Unfortunately, many pastors neglect this training because they not only lack confidence in their teaching abilities but in their *own* leadership abilities. Since many do not identify leadership as one of their gifts, they pull back from providing the needed training. In many cases pastors may feel that training lay people is a classic case of the blind leading the blind.

This book is designed to help you equip your lay leaders to lead. The principles shared will give you the information needed to teach basic leadership skills to those you have the opportunity to serve.

My goal is to provide you and your lay leaders with principles that will form a firm foundation for taking on increased responsibility in the life of your church. I encourage you as you teach leadership to those you lead, who in turn will lead others. These foundational principles will enable them to lead more effectively not only in your church, but also in their family, place of employment, and community.

1 BECOME AN INFLUENCER

If your actions inspire others to dream more, learn more, do more and become more, you are a leader.

John Quincy Adams

Influence is a critical component of leadership. Those we train to be leaders must understand the significant role influence plays in leading people. Because people respond much more readily to those they trust, effective leaders must spend a great deal of time gaining the trust of the people they want to influence. Influence is a by-product of trust.

Influence is the power to affect others positively or negatively. Everybody has *some* influence, but the scope may vary. Some people influence thousands, some dozens, others only one or two. It is not the scope but the significance of the effects that matter. Never allow yourself or the people you teach to ask, "Do I have influence?" They do! Instead they should ask, "How will I utilize the influence I have?"

8

The goal of being an effective leader is to have positive influence. We are to involve ourselves in the lives of others in such a way that we can enable them to realize their full potential, a potential that is ultimately rooted in Jesus Christ. Our influence can and should draw this out of them. Leadership is a form of discipleship. We influence others so that they might influence those with whom we may never come in contact.

HOW WE INFLUENCE

Influence is often more an art than a science. It is something we learn by emulating those who have impacted us and by skills we develop along the way. There are two understandings that will enable us in the development of our influence: (1) Influence is *who we are, not what we do,* and (2) influence is a *choice*, not a *chance*.

INFLUENCE IS WHO WE ARE, NOT WHAT WE DO

When I was in high school, Dale Bailey, my youth pastor, was extremely influential in my life because of the time he shared with me. I don't remember all the specific things he shared, but I do remember the kind of man he was. His impact on my life was a result of his character, not his title.

> Make a list of three people who have influenced you. Take a moment to write them a note of appreciation.

9

Most of our influence will occur because of the kind of people we become. Therefore, as we strive to be influencers, we must understand our "who." Paul places a high priority on understanding ourselves. In 1 Timothy 4:16 he instructs Timothy, "Keep a close watch on how you live and on your teaching . . ." The New American Standard Version states it this way: "Pay close attention to yourself . . ." It is interesting to note that Paul is more concerned with Timothy's life than with his teaching. Teaching lessons without a lifestyle that reflects those lessons is counterproductive. Who we are— more than what we say—will influence those around us.

We must pay attention to ourselves. It is to our benefit to understand ourselves, for self-perception will dictate our leadership. Simple knowledge of our personality could enhance our leadership influence tremendously.

Dan Fouts was the quarterback of the San Diego Chargers in the late seventies and early eighties. He is in the top five quarterbacks for total passing yardage in the history of the NFL, and he was adept at pulling out wins from the mouth of defeat.

Inside the huddle, Fouts had the ability to inspire his team. No matter what the score, no matter what the odds, he instilled inspiration that propelled those around him to another level. He influenced out of his innate unwilling-ness to accept defeat. You can influence your huddle through four simple actions:

1. Put more into life than you take out.
Les Brown, a former state legislator, once said: "Shoot for the moon. Even if you miss it, you'll land among the stars." Attack life! Develop your potential and invest in people. Aim for the stars of involvement, encouragement, faith, hope, love, and laughter.

2. Have a singleness of purpose.
Approach leadership with a rifle, not a shotgun. A shot-gun sprays its shot; it hits many things. A rifle is more direct and accurate. As a leader you cannot do everything, but you can do something. So do one thing well—and do it really well!

3. Develop deep integrity.
Integrity has been defined as who you are when no one is looking. Your private self, sooner or later, will spill over into your public self. The deeper your private life, the stronger your public life. Allow God into your inner life "because the Spirit who lives in you is greater than the spirit who lives in the world" (1 John 4:4).

4. Strive for proper motivation.

The famous missionary Hudson Taylor founded the China Inland Mission. Prior to his involvement in missions, missionary organizations focused their work on the coastal regions of China. Taylor wanted to take the gospel to the people who never ventured to the coast. The impact of his vision continues today.

I have heard that when Taylor made the decision to enter missionary work, his brother tried to talk him out of it. He wanted Hudson to stay home and go into business with him. His brother told him essentially that if he went, he would amount to nothing. But Hudson went anyway.

> We are the sum total, good or bad, of the choices we make.

Ironically, the inscription on this same brother's tombstone tells us something about what really stands the test of time. It reads: "Here lies the brother of Hudson Taylor."

Obedience to God is the only proper motivation. Hudson Taylor followed the call of God. Hudson's brother followed after fame and fortune. Who is remembered?

INFLUENCE IS A CHOICE, NOT A CHANCE

In the early days of television, "The Ed Sullivan Show" was the one gig entertainers valued most. A successful outing on Mr. Sullivan's show was a guarantee of future greatness, much like the "Tonight Show with Jay Leno" is today. Sullivan's stamp of approval could translate into many opportunities because of his influence as the entertainment power broker of the 1950s and 60s.

Jackie Mason was a bright, young comedian in the 1960s. He was excited to have a spot on this nationally televised show. He had confidence in his routine and this was the break he had worked years to gain. This was to be his catapult into the big time!

Ed Sullivan gave a glowing introduction to this "fine, fine young man." The curtain went up, the lights came on, and Jackie hit the stage running. The audience loved him! Everything he did brought strong laughter.

During part of his routine he began to use hand gestures. The audience responded so well he began to ad lib. A finger gesture here. A quick flick of the finger there. The audience roared its approval.

Mr. Sullivan was not laughing. In fact, he was downright disgusted. He motioned for the director to switch to a commercial. When the commercial ended and the regular show resumed, Jackie Mason was not only off the stage—he was about to embark on a fight for his entertainment life.

What had happened? In the midst of his "finger" humor, Mr. Sullivan thought Jackie Mason had made an obscene gesture to his studio and home audience. Ed Sullivan refused to tolerate that kind of behavior and ejected Mason from his show.

It took Jackie Mason twenty years to recover from that incident—twenty years to recover what he lost in one minute. Our choices have a great affect on our ability to influence.

Choice, not chance, determines our leadership. Right choices and positive corresponding actions enhance our ability to influence others. We are the sum total, good or bad, of the choices we make. Decisions dictate actions. Choices made at the beginning determine, to a great extent, end results. Daniel is an excellent example of this principle.

Daniel was best known for his lack of fear in the face of great danger—a lion's den filled with certain death. The Old Testament tells us that he was forced into this predicament because of his unwillingness to give up his allegiance to the one true God.

14

We must admire a man of his character and faith. How would you respond if placed in a similar situation—a situation where you had to choose between potential death and your relationship with God? Daniel had a faith that should humble and challenge us. Could we respond in such a manner?

Encouragement comes when we take a complete look at Daniel's life. The Daniel of chapter six must be seen in light of chapter one. What Daniel did in chapter one sets the tone for the rest of his life.

Daniel had just been taken into captivity by the Babylonian King Nebuchadnezzar (Dan. 1:1–4). The Babylonians had overrun Jerusalem and had captured the sharpest and brightest young men. The plan was to indoctrinate them for use in positions of leadership.

It was during this time that the foundation for greatness was laid: Daniel made an initial choice not to fall into the trap. Daniel 1:8 (NASB) says, "But Daniel *made up his mind* . . ." (emphasis added).

Yes, Daniel made a choice. He made up his mind. He developed a resolution. It was his godly decision in chapter one to stay true to the law of God, which set him up as one of God's great men in chapter six. It was the early

15

"making up of his mind" that enabled him to act as he did when confronted with a den of hungry lions. The choices he made in the easy times helped him lead in the tough times.

The early choices for Daniel resulted in his ability to influence others. In Daniel 6 we discover how he influenced those in his sphere.

1. He influenced through consistency in living (verses 3–4). Fellow administrators and satraps were jealous of Daniel. They wanted to find some kind of charge against him. Yet we are told, ". . . they couldn't find anything to criticize or condemn. He was faithful, always responsible, and completely trustworthy" (verse 4).

We may not be perfect in our leadership, but we can be consistent. Consistency in our conduct and decision making inspires those we lead to confidence. They know we teach what we are, and we are what we teach. When we show ourselves dependable, we increase in our credibility. Confidence and credibility positively influence those we lead.

2. He influenced through his spiritual life (verse 10). The administrators and satraps knew the only part of Daniel's life that might get him into trouble would be his

16

faith. They tricked the king into issuing a decree that would require all people to worship only him for the next thirty days. Daniel listened to the edict and "he went home and knelt down *as usual* in his upstairs room, with its windows opened toward Jerusalem. He prayed three times a day, just as he had *always done* . . ." (verse 10, emphasis added).

His spirituality was not dependent on his circumstances or the crowd. He followed God because it was the right thing to do, not because it was convenient or popular. When those we lead sense authenticity in our spiritual lives, our influence is increased. It's not that we have all the answers, but we have confidence in the one who does. When it comes to spiritual confidence, it's not *what* you know, but *who* you know.

3. He influenced through hope (verse 16).
King Darius liked Daniel, but he had been caught in a deception so he was forced to abide by his own decree. Even though Daniel had to go to the lion's den, his faith gave him hope. Notice the hope that Darius sensed in Daniel. "'May your God, whom you serve so faithfully, rescue you'" (verse 16). Daniel trusted in His God. The hope he carried with him into the lion's den rubbed off on Darius.

In September 1988, Hurricane Gilbert hit the Louisiana coast. At that time it was considered the "storm of the century." It battered the shoreline, severely disrupting the shrimping business. Many shrimp boats were lost, causing great concern for several families dependent on shrimping for their livelihood.

On the morning news I watched an interview with a shrimp boat owner. He was asked how the storm would impact the shrimpers. With the devastation of Gilbert as a backdrop, this man said, "Well, there is a good side. The storm will have stirred up the bottom of the ocean, making for better shrimping once we're able to get back out there." This man understood hope!

People look to us for hope. Hope is encouragement in discouraging times; the belief that there is always a way. It opens people's eyes to the potential in problems and the opportunities in obstacles. Hope is the empty tomb—we need to be "empty tomb" leaders. That is, we never leave our people at the despair of the crucifixion, but move them toward the mouth of the open grave!

INFLUENCE INFUSERS

Joe was a great believer in people. His faith in and optimism about others helped launch them to greatness. He was an influencer.

Who was Joe? He was Barnabas, the "Son of Encouragement." We are introduced to him in Acts 4:36 as "Joseph, the one the apostles nicknamed Barnabas (which means 'Son of Encouragement')." Barnabas has much to teach us about influencing others.

1. Be generous with what you have (Acts 4:37).
We read that Barnabas "sold a field . . . and brought the money to the apostles." He shared what he had. Leaders need to be generous with what they have. Time, talent, ideas, insights—whatever it is, share it liberally with those you serve.

2. Believe the best of people (Acts 9:27).
Saul had persecuted the Christians for many months. He focused on crushing this upstart "cult." When he was converted, few were willing to jump on his bandwagon. Most felt it was a trick—a way to flush out the followers of "The Way."

There was one who stepped alongside him, one person who put his reputation and life on the line. This one was Barnabas. He went to bat for Saul. He told Saul's story to the others. He was the one who sold them on the reality of the persecutor's conversion. Barnabas believed in Saul because he believed in people.

3. Encourage people (Acts 11:22–23).

Good things were happening in the church. In Antioch, people were coming to the Lord in large numbers. Those in Jerusalem wanted to give them encouragement. Who did they send? Barnabas, of course. He went and encouraged them "to stay true to the Lord" (verse 23).

People need to be encouraged. They need someone to recognize the good things they do. It doesn't take much creativity to criticize, but it does take effort to find the positive. I once heard it said that when people go mining for gold, they have to remove many tons of dirt to find just a little gold. However, they never go looking for dirt, only gold. Encouraging people is like looking for gold. Don't get discouraged when you encounter dirt—keep digging.

4. Invest yourself in others (Acts 11:25–30).

Scripture tells us that "both [Saul and Barnabas] stayed there with the church for a full year, teaching large crowds of people . . ." (verse 26). Barnabas invested himself in Saul. I believe that if it weren't for Barnabas, Saul might not have become the great apostle Paul. Barnabas nurtured Paul, poured his life into him and helped him mature. The apostle Paul was the return on the investment that encourager Barnabas made in persecutor Saul.

In August 1995, the church I pastored made the decision to do a major renovation on our thirty-five-year-old sanctuary. The first step was to put together a crew of people to do internal demolition. Around forty people showed up to take care of this task.

Dust was everywhere as we ripped up carpet, knocked out walls, tore down ceilings, and dismantled the platform. There were people of all shapes, sizes, and ages. It was a wonderful project for individuals like me because absolutely no skill was needed. It doesn't take much training to destroy something.

When this phase was completed, the remodeling began. This was the part that required skilled and trained people—those who knew how to construct, build, and refurbish. Their task was much more difficult and it took much longer than the demolition.

Anybody can tear down, but not everyone can build up. It doesn't take a genius to destroy something, but it does take some know-how to construct something of value. The unskilled can quickly take apart that which takes the skilled a lot of time to put together.

Do you build or demolish? Influential leaders always leave people better than they found them.

BECOME AN INFLUENCER

KEY POINTS

- Put more into life than you take out, have a singleness of purpose, develop deep integrity, and strive for proper motivation.
- We influence others through consistent living, a deep spiritual life, and overflowing hope.
- Influence infusers are generous with what they have, believe the best of people, encourage those around them, and invest themselves in others.

DISCUSSION QUESTIONS

1. Who is in your "influence huddle?"

2. What area of your life needs to be more consistent?

3. How are you currently developing your spiritual life?

4. What do you do to inspire hope in others?

ACTION STEPS

1. List your top five strengths. What might you do to lead from your strengths?

2. Review Daniel 6:3–16. Evaluate your life and determine where you may need to make improvements.

3. List three people to whom you can be a Barnabas. Next to each name, write how you might be a Barnabas to them. Over the next week display that Barnabas action toward them.

RESOURCES

- Florence Littauer—*Personality Plus*
- Albert L. Winseman, Donald Clifton, Curt Liesveld—*Living Your Strengths*
- Jack Lynn—*Clear Vision*
- Norman Vincent Peale—*Why Some Positive Thinkers Get Powerful Results*

2 SERVE OTHERS

It is one of the most beautiful compensations of this life that no man can sincerely try to help another without helping himself.

Ralph Waldo Emerson

The servant-leader model isn't a new idea. Jesus modeled it for us over two thousand years ago. In His ministry, Jesus made it clear that He did not come to be served, but to serve. "But among you it will be different. Whoever wants to be a leader among you must be your servant, and whoever wants to be first among you must be the slave of everyone else. For even the Son of Man came not to be served but to serve others and give his life as a ransom for many" (Mark 10:43–45).

Most leaders struggle with this model. The struggle is not with the principle, but with its practice. It is hard to understand what it really means to be a servant and lead at the same time. Most models of leadership show a pyramid with the leader at the pinnacle. Organizational charts put the leader at the head and illustrate the others as "subservient" to him or her. But Jesus inverted the pyramid and threw the organizational charts of His day into disarray. He advocated humility and servanthood. You may struggle with His challenge, but you cannot argue with His success as a leader.

When I attempt to grab hold of servant-leadership, I often rebel. What does it mean for me to be a servant? Must I cater to the whims and fancies of those I lead? Is my only priority serving others, or are there other things I can put before their needs? Why even bother to plan and strategize? Someone will just come along with a need and I'll have to drop everything to help them. As a leader I cannot do everything, but servant-leadership seems to dictate that I must be all things to all men.

Servant-leadership has no easy implementation plan. It is one thing to understand the model of Jesus, but quite another to master it. A good starting point is to study how Jesus put His own principle into practice. A remarkable example of servant-leadership is found in the thirteenth chapter of the Gospel of John.

> A servant-leader sees a need and takes personal responsibility to meet that need with the resources available.

25

In this passage, Jesus lives out a working definition of servant-leadership: a servant-leader is someone who sees a need and takes personal responsibility to meet that need with the resources available. Keeping this description in mind, let's walk through John 13:2–17.

You will be unable to practice servant-leadership until you have a strong sense of self. Hear what John says about Jesus. "Jesus knew that the Father had given him authority over everything and that he had come from God and would return to God" (verse 3).

Jesus knew who He was; He knew where His power rested. Jesus was humble in the truest sense of the word. He knew His strengths, but refused to flaunt them. He could serve because He was not dependent on others for His self-worth or strength.

When Jesus saw the need—His disciples' dirty feet—He took the initiative. His internal strength overcame the external barrier of appearance. How His actions appeared to His disciples did not matter. What mattered was that there was a need and He wanted to meet it.

26

If we are going to truly serve others, we must have confidence in the person God has created us to be. Inward focus blurs outward sight. Worry over what others might think, concern over how something might appear, or if someone of our "station" should be doing it will hinder our ability to serve. Service is the result of our relationship with God. As Chuck Colson has said, "In right relationship with our Creator, knowing we belong to Him, we pour ourselves out in service to others."

Jesus gathered the necessary resources. "So he got up from the table, took off his robe, wrapped a towel around his waist, and poured water into a basin. Then he began to wash the disciples' feet, drying them with the towel he had around him" (verses 4–5).

Jesus got a towel, a pitcher of water and a basin; He gathered exactly what He needed to meet the present need. It would have done Jesus no good to attempt to wash the disciples' feet if He had neither water to clean them, nor a towel to dry them.

Servant-leadership is not merely observing needs, but meeting those needs with the resources available. When needs arise, the leader must find the means to address them. Do your people need teaching materials? Provide them. Do your people need encouragement? Give it to them. Do your people need your time? Spend it with them. Whatever the need, find a way to meet it.

27

✻ *Jesus made it clear that what He did was done as an example.* "After washing their feet, he put on his robe again and sat down and asked, 'Do you understand what I was doing? You call me "Teacher" and "Lord," and you are right, because that's what I am. And since I, your Lord and Teacher, have washed your feet, you ought to wash each other's feet. I have given you an example to follow. Do as I have done to you'" (verses 12–15).

When Jesus was done washing their feet, He went back to where He had been. His goal was not merely to wash His disciples' feet, but to show them how to serve. It was not His purpose to wash feet; He was to go to the cross. Clean feet were a definite need, but to spend all of His time meeting that need would have kept Him from His ultimate act of service. Jesus desired to prepare His disciples to wash feet so He could wash their hearts of sin.

There are times when servant-leadership dictates that you set aside what you are doing to help train others. Your own agenda may have to wait. Time spent modeling ministry for others is always an investment, never an intrusion.

28 On an episode of the television program "E.R.," an intern was asked if he had ever done a certain medical procedure. The intern responded that he had seen one done, but had never done one himself. The teaching doctor

looked at him and confidently said, "See one, do one, teach one. Now it's your chance."

There it is—a simple, but effective strategy of training others to minister. It's how Jesus instructed His disciples. *See one*, "And since I . . . have washed your feet . . ." (verse 14); *Do one*, ". . . you ought to wash each other's feet" (verse 14); *Teach one*, "I have given you an example to follow. Do as I have done to you" (verse 15).

Servant-leadership is much more than doing for others; it is helping others do for themselves. If we approach each day looking for opportunities to meet needs and help others learn to meet needs, we put ourselves in position to experience authentic leadership—a leadership that will attract followers, accomplish goals, and accentuate vision.

WHY SERVE?

Servant-leadership prepares us for a lifestyle of selflessness. Most of life centers around us. We expect our people and products to cater to our needs and wants. Advertising barrages us with messages of what we "deserve" and how certain products will provide it. How often we catch ourselves saying, "That's not fair!" In our search for fairness and gaining all that we deserve, it is easy to become self-centered.

Developing our servant-leadership style enables us to remove "self" from the center and replace it with "others." Success is redefined from what is gained to what is given. As Denis Waitley has said in his book *The Double Win*, "Winning (success) is taking the talent or potential you were born with, and have since developed, and using it fully toward a goal or purpose that makes you happy and simultaneously serves other people."

Servant-leadership provides motivation. It motivates not only the leader, but also those who are being led. When they realize that someone else is concerned about them, their sense of value and self-worth is increased. People of value want to set and reach goals. They know they are not going through life alone. There is another who cares about them and their hopes for the future—one who is available to help them reach their goals.

> The true spiritual leader is concerned infinitely more with the service he can render God and his fellowmen than with the benefits and pleasures he can extract from life.
>
> J. Oswald Sanders

I remember hearing a story about a famous film producer. As a child, he had a fight with another boy and lost. While his mother was bathing his black eye, he told her how it was entirely the fault of the other boy. It was the other boy who had started the fight, he claimed.

His mother said nothing, but when the first aid was completed, she took her son to the back door of their home. Nearby were several hills that created a fine echo. She told him to call those hills all the bad names he could think of. He did so and the bad names all came back to him.

"Now," she said, as the story goes, "Call out, 'God bless you.'" He did so and back came, "God bless you."

The movie producer never forgot that lesson. What you give to others you get back from them.

How do you motivate others with your leadership? Do you motivate them with the negative and the destructive? Or do you serve them and help them become servants through the positive and the instructive? What you give is what you get. The echo you may be getting could be your own.

Servant-leadership produces other leaders. Jesus produced people who led the church with faith, humility, and a tremendous willingness to risk. He taught them how to serve by serving them. When He became involved in their lives, their desire to pass on His love was magnified. Personal involvement results in a productive increase.

Bob Richards was an Olympic champion in the pole vault. He was willing to work hard and do whatever it took to accomplish the goals he had set for himself. He had his sights set on the record that was held by Dutch Warmer Dam. He was almost a foot short of the record-breaking height. He sensed he had leveled off. He just couldn't seem to get any higher, so he decided to call Dutch Warmer Dam and ask for his help.

Dutch welcomed the opportunity and invited Richards to come and visit him. They spent three days together. During those three days Dutch gave him everything he had. He provided insight into things he was doing wrong and gave Bob methods of correcting them. As a result of those three days, Bob Richards increased his pole vaulting height by eight inches.

Reflecting back on that experience, Bob Richards observed, "I've found that sports champions and heroes willingly do this just to help you become great, too."

Great servant-leaders will help others get what they need so that they, too, can succeed.

32

Outward looking—instead of inward staring—enhances personal health while helping others at the same time. Build up your people. Invest your time in them and help them grow. This is servant-leadership.

The servant-leader is dedicated to accomplishing tasks regardless of who gets the credit. Leaders who are more concerned about personal recognition than building the people they lead will encounter frustration and futility in their leadership.

Mother Teresa was attending a party full of dignitaries. The guest list included presidents and statesmen from around the world. They came in their crowns and jewels and silks. Mother Teresa wore her ever-present sari, held together by a safety pin.

She was engaged in conversation with a nobleman who was intrigued by her work to the

> True leadership must be for the benefit of the followers not the enrichment of the leaders.
>
> Unknown

poorest of the poor in Calcutta. From his vantage point, her work seemed endless and frustrating. He asked her if she didn't become discouraged by seeing so few successes.

"No, I do not become discouraged," Mother Teresa answered. "You see, God has not called me to a ministry of success. He has called me to a ministry of mercy."

Mother Teresa understood that it was not what she got out of it, but what those she served received. Recognition and "success" did not drive her; mercy and compassion did. She had seen needs and taken personal responsibility to meet those needs with the resources she had.

CHARACTERISTICS OF A SERVANT-LEADER

Knowing what you are looking for increases your ability to recognize and identify the object. The same is true for servant-leadership. Having an idea of what it looks like enhances our ability to attain it. What are some characteristics of servant-leaders?

A servant-leader creates ways to get things done, instead of criticizing what is undone. As we mentioned last chapter, it doesn't take much effort to point out a problem, but it does take insight to solve problems.

When the Titanic hit the iceberg, the last thing the passengers needed was people criticizing the steering of the ship. What they needed were people who could create ways to save lives.

The saying goes that the people who insist things can't be done get messed up by those doing them. Servant-leaders waste little effort on the "cant's" and focus on the "cans."

In one of the houses where my family lived, there was an inner room that my wife wanted to use as a family room. She wanted to place our long couch in the room. I looked at the couch. I analyzed the angle of the corners, determining if I could navigate the couch into that particular room. With authority I declared, "There is no way that couch is going into that room."

"There must be a way," Joni insisted.

"No way!" I continued confidently. "That couch is not fitting through the door into that room. The angle is too drastic."

"There must be a way. There is always a way."

"If you can get that couch in the room," I said, "I'll take you out to dinner."

> The person in places of authority must assume the attitude of a servant.
>
> —Alan Loy McGinnis

I should never have offered dinner. Right after throwing down the glove of challenge I was off to another project. When I returned, Joni and her sister were sitting triumphantly in the room on the couch. I had criticized, but Joni and her sister had created. The job got done!

SERVE OTHERS

Servant-leaders move ahead, instead of moan from behind. I am reminded of the story of a woman whose car stalled at a signal light. She tried desperately to get the engine to turn over, but the car would not start.

Behind her an impatient, hurried man began honking his horn as soon as the light changed to green. The more she attempted to start her car, the more he honked. Finally, after several minutes of listening to this obnoxious horn, the woman got out of her car and walked to the man behind her.

Pulling open his door, she said, "Listen, I'm tired. Why don't you try to start my car and I'll sit back here and honk at you!"

A servant-leader would have gotten out and tried to help. A honk, a moan, or a complaint from behind never encourages progress. Movement, not moaning, changes situations.

Servant-leaders apply themselves to helping, instead of avoiding times to help. There are many people who, when work has to be done, seem to have a reason why they can't pitch in. They don't have the time. They don't have the talent. They don't have . . . well, they don't have whatever is needed.

36

Another anecdote tells of a salesman who called his wife from a coin-operated telephone in a distant city. He had just said good-bye to her and replaced the receiver. As he was walking away, the phone rang. He went back and answered it. He was expecting to be informed of extra charges. Instead, the operator said, "I thought you'd like to know. Just after you hung up your wife said, 'I love you.'" The operator applied herself to helping. She could have ignored this situation. She could have found several reasons to do nothing. Instead, she characterized a servant-leader attitude and invested in the life of another.

MAKING SERVANT-LEADERSHIP WORK

The concept of servant-leadership, as mentioned earlier, is easily understood but not easily put into practice. What are some practical applications we can make to being a servant-leader? Following are four ways of putting servant-leadership to work on a daily basis.

1. Make the choice.

Choose to be a servant-leader (Phil. 2:6–7). Jesus "gave up his divine privileges; he took the humble position of a slave" (verse 7). It was His choice. He could have demanded His rights as God; instead He relinquished those rights to mingle with humanity.

37

2. Apply the MPFI principle.

The MPFI principle stands for *Make People Feel Important*. People like to feel appreciated. This is especially true in volunteer organizations such as the church. The people we lead are not in it for financial gain, community recognition, or increased social status. They are active in ministry in order to bring glory to God. However, as leaders, we have the task of helping them feel important.

Bob Newhart is an actor/comedian who has developed this principle to an art form. He has made a living at giving others recognition. In all of the sitcoms in which he has starred, the comedy seems to surround him more than point to him. He is like a ringmaster caught in the center ring, with co-stars moving in and out, seemingly stealing the laughs and the show; he simply tries to manage the chaos. Time magazine once said of him, "Newhart, as usual, seems happy to share the spotlight."

3. Emphasize the goal, not the glory.

Personal gain is not a part of servant-leadership. Servant-leaders desire team accomplishment over individual achievement. Lead people to a goal. Share in the journey. Enjoy the sense of fulfillment that a shared goal provides.

38

4. Release those you lead to success.

Leaders who serve find great satisfaction in watching those they lead grow, change, and stretch. They understand the truth of the statement, "Success without a successor is failure." Jesus needed the disciples to carry on the message of the gospel. He provided the example; He empowered them with the Holy Spirit; He commanded them to make disciples. But He still needed them to move out with the good news.

Lead people to success by releasing them to it. Give them the key. Provide them with whatever they need to be all they can be.

KNOWING WHEN TO HELP

No one can meet every need. How do you decide which needs to address and which to encourage someone else to meet? It is impossible to meet every need you encounter. Here are some questions that will enable you to make intelligent choices:

- The assessment question: Is there a real need?
- The availability question: Can I be part of the solution?
- The attitude question: What is keeping me from helping?
- The ability question: What can I do?
- The action question: What will I do?

- Servant leaders see needs, gather resources, and take action.
- Serving others removes pride, provides motivation for humility, and produces other leaders.
- Servant leaders create options, move ahead, and apply themselves to helping.
- Put servant-leadership to work by making good choices, applying the MPFI principle, emphasizing the goal (not the glory), and releasing people to success.

DISCUSSION QUESTIONS

1. What hinders your servant leadership?

2. What might you do to serve better?

ACTION STEPS

1. Identify situations in which you tend to be the most critical. Determine what causes the critical mindset, and give it over to the Lord in prayer.

40

2. Make someone feel important today. Be creative.

3. Write a note of appreciation to someone who has recently helped you out.

SERVE OTHERS

RESOURCES

- Charles Colson—*Who Speaks for God?*
- Denis Waitley—*The Double Win*
- Alice Gray—*Stories for the Heart*
- Wayne Schmidt—*Lead On*

3 **COMMUNICATE CLEARLY**

> *You can have brilliant ideas, but if you can't get them across, your ideas won't get you anywhere.*
>
> Lee Iacocca

*A*esop's Fables tells the story of an argument between the North Wind and the Sun. Each thought himself stronger than the other. To settle the discussion they decided on a contest of strength. The contest would be to see who could cause a passing wayfarer to strip off his clothing.

The North Wind went first. He began to blow, but the harder he blew the tighter the traveler drew his clothes around him. Not wanting to lose the contest, the North Wind increased his assault. But when the man began to put on more clothing to protect himself from the cold, the North Wind gave up.

The Sun then stepped up to take his turn. He glowed gently, just above the horizon. This warming trend caused the man to remove the extra clothing he had added against the cold. The Sun made a slow climb, shining more brightly as he climbed higher in the sky. The wayfarer, unable to bear the heat, stripped off his clothes and jumped into a nearby river.

The ability to communicate is vital if we are to be effective leaders. And as the fable illustrates, it is not what you communicate so much as how you communicate that counts. The Sun won the competition because warm encouragement wins over abrasive prodding every time. The North Wind got the attention of the traveler, but his mode of communication did not result in accomplishing the goal. The Sun was able to get the traveler's attention and achieve the desired result. Good communicators gain both attention and results.

Communication is the ability to make the complicated sim-

> Communication is the ability to make the complicated simple.

ple. Leaders who are able to explain things, clarify situations, and lay out a clear course of action instill confidence in those they lead. It is the one who communicates clearly that changes the world.

Ronald Reagan was a superb communicator. History recognizes him to be one of the greatest communicators of all the United States' presidents. He restored faith in

43

America. He enhanced national self-esteem. He made it "all right" to be patriotic and have pride in this great nation. Much of this was the result of his ability to communicate to the American people.

Conversely, if you are unable or unwilling to communicate to those you lead, plan to struggle. Nothing undermines the confidence of people like a leader who doesn't effectively communicate with them. Incomplete information, lack of openness, and misunderstood facts breed an environment of mistrust.

Communication goes beyond what we say or write. It spills over into who we are. Genuine communicators do not merely expose thoughts, but model what they share. Leadership demands that we act in accordance with what we communicate.

The movie *Gettysburg* is an excellent commentary on leadership. On both sides of the battle, the leaders needed to motivate their men to action. The goal of the leader was to communicate that their cause was worth dying for and get their men to act. However, nothing communicated this message more clearly than when the leaders drew their swords and charged into battle first! Their actions communicated very clearly what they said.

DO PEOPLE UNDERSTAND THE WORDS COMING OUT OF YOUR MOUTH?

You cannot lead if you are unable to communicate. You may have a great deal to say; you may have a wonderful message; you may have an intense passion that you want to declare. However, the inability to clearly pass along what you want will result in frustration for both you and those you lead. Your frustration will be the result of not getting the response you desire. Their frustration will come from their inability to figure out what you want.

Communication comes from the Latin word *communis*. It literally means "common." The essence of communication is to establish common ground with those with whom we are communicating. It is on this common ground that we can construct the framework necessary to bring about understanding. There are three primary ways people communicate: verbally, in writing, and with images.

Say It

Leaders must hone their skills in the area of public speaking. Following are six practical tips that will increase your effectiveness in the public arena.

1. Be believable.

Don't share what you do not really believe. People can tell

if you are genuinely interested in a topic or just putting out information. Your topic will not be exciting to your audience if it is not exciting to you.

I had an English professor at San Diego State University who loved words. She did not teach as much as she simply shared her passion for the English language both verbal and written. She was an older woman, more like a grandmother than a college professor.

Each class time she would read words and definitions from a dictionary. The words were treated with tenderness. Her voice was filled with an awe of their beauty. I thought maybe she had a "special" dictionary. It certainly could not be like the ones I had used. Never had I experienced such an encounter with defined words. I would leave her class wanting to spend time in dictionary devotional reading.

She communicated to us because she was believable. "Believability" is the direct result of living that which you communicate. It is feeling something deeply. You may not necessarily understand all that you are communicating, as much as you are sharing what you are discovering.

46

2. Know your audience.

With whom are you communicating? Talking to children

differs from speaking to teenagers, which differs from sharing with adults. What is said and how it is said should not be dictated by what the information is, but by the audience addressed. I heard Fred Smith, a marvelous leader and layman, put it this way at a conference: "You talk to an audience about a subject, you never talk about a subject to an audience."

These three questions may be helpful in enabling you to know the audience you are addressing:

- **Who are they?** As best you can, establish their ages, backgrounds, experience levels, and what, if any, information they have about what you are sharing.
- **Where are they from?** Were they made to come? Do they really want to be there to learn? Perhaps they came for the party afterwards, and you have to be endured (like vegetables before dessert).
- **What do they need?** Do they need encouragement? Exhortation? Solid teaching? An opportunity to laugh?

Meeting the needs of an audience does not mean being unprepared. It doesn't mean you walk into the group you are addressing, get the feel of the environment, and shoot from the hip. In reality, you must become even better pre-pared. The better you know your material, the more readily you will be able to adapt to the situations you encounter.

When you know what you want to say and are well-prepared, you will be able to communicate with any audience in such a manner that everyone will walk away with something. The late J. Vernon McGee, a renowned radio preacher, liked to say, "I like to put the cookies on the bottom shelf. That way, everyone can reach them."

3. Share yourself.

Give people a part of you to take with them. Those you lead need to identify with you. They do not want a performance or a personality; they want a person—a person who laughs, cries, and struggles with life, yet who has discovered God is here.

Share personal stories as illustrations. Each time I have done this, I have had someone in the audience approach me and share a similar experience. When people identify with you, they identify with your God. And when people begin to identify with God, lives are changed.

4. Prepare well.

Bobby Knight, the Texas Tech basketball coach, says, "The will to succeed is important, but what's more important is the will to prepare." There is no excuse for lack of preparation. Study tools are plentiful. The availability of resources is higher than it has ever been. The single biggest barrier to preparation is the inability or unwillingness to discipline one's time.

We must *take* the time to *make* the time to prepare. No one else can do this for you. Most people will want to steal your time. I urge you to protect this limited resource. Set aside a time to prepare. Keep it as a non-negotiable.

5. Be enjoyable.

People ought to enjoy hearing what you have to say. Their enjoyment level will increase as you salt your teachings with principles, illustrations, and humor. Principles give people hooks on which to hang the truth in the everyday. Illustrations are keys that unlock the doors to practical application. Humor is the sugarcoating that helps people swallow hard truth.

The goal of communication is not merely to convince people, but to change them. Give people principles. Color the principles with illustrations. Provide people with laughter. Soon they will be convinced they need to change.

6. Be empowered.

Ultimately, God will be the one to drive the message

home. It will be His Spirit that will nudge the hearts of the listeners in their areas of need. We must do what we can humanly and leave the rest to God.

Write It

Matt was a young man in whom I saw a lot of potential. He had just begun to attend the church where I was ministering. I wrote him a short note. In it I told him that I believed he had great potential as a leader.

Years later, Matt was on a missions trip with me. We started talking, when out of the blue he said, "Do you remember the note you sent me? The one about you seeing leadership potential in me?"

I had a vague recollection of the note, so I smiled and gave him a positive response.

He went on, "I have kept that note all these years. It encouraged me. It has proven to be a continual source of motivation for me."

Writing carries an incredible impact. People enjoy receiving something especially for them. A handwritten note or letter is something people can hold, re-read, and use as a reminder that someone cares about them. Writing can make a difference in the lives of others. It takes very little to let those you lead know you care. You can tell them out loud, but when you write it down, it can be savored time and time again.

When writing, practice the "Four Cs." These provide a great pattern to follow regardless of the length or type of written communication.

> Clarity: Does it make sense?
> Continuity: Does it fit together?
> Concise: Are you getting to the point?
> Content: Did you have something to say?

Show It

People communicate through images. Images such as body language, facial expressions, pictures, and videos are usually combined with verbal and written communication. The more adept we are at utilizing images, the better we'll be able to communicate. We are a visually-oriented society. Painting images—whether through speaking, writing, or through an object lesson—enhances people's abilities to own what is being communicated.

When I was the youth pastor at Skyline Wesleyan, I had the opportunity to preach at one of the morning services. My

51

sermon was about hope. At the conclusion of the service, I shared a story I had heard about a poor family whose young son desperately wanted a kite. They couldn't afford to purchase one, so his mother gently kept putting him off.

One evening, as she was getting her son ready for bed, he looked up at her and declared, "Since we cannot afford a kite, I'm going to ask God for one." He prayed a simple prayer of faith. His mom tucked him in and left the room wondering how she would explain why God couldn't provide him with a kite.

The next morning, she opened the shade of the kitchen window. Dangling from their tree, right outside the window, was a yellow kite. Astonished, she ran upstairs to get her son. That yellow kite became a symbol to them of God's provision. The catch phrase was, "When hope seems the dimmest, God sends a yellow kite."

Before the sermon began, I stationed a high school student far above the congregation in a spotlight bay. This particular bay was in such a location that if attention was drawn to it, the entire congregation could easily view it. When I got to the part of the story where the mother opened the shade and saw the kite, I had the student lower a yellow kite. By a gesture of my hand I directed the congregation's attention skyward. The response to the story was wonderfully enhanced by seeing a real yellow kite dangling from the sanctuary ceiling.

That was an image—a simple method to embed in the minds of those listening the truth of what was being communicated. To this day, people who were there remember the image. Communication is getting a message across. Work at developing your communication skills because the ability to communicate enhances the ability to lead. People rally behind that which they can understand and grasp. Communication is the leader's method of providing understanding.

BE WHAT YOU SAY

Our lifestyle communicates a message to those we lead. Leaders must go beyond simply teaching lessons; they must be examples of what they teach. Leaders reproduce who they are. As one adage puts it, "The only thing that walks back from a tomb with the mourners and refuses to be buried is character." What we say will be forgotten, but what we are will survive us.

In the early 1970s, the office of the United States Presidency was tainted like never before in history. It was the result of a break-in that would be known from that time on simply as "Watergate." Out of this event came many personalities.

People who would have never been brought to the public's attention became national celebrities. G. Gordon Liddy was one of these individuals.

In an interview on "Sun-Up San Diego," a local talk show, I heard him explain something that has relevance to leaders. He said: "Each of us has two parts: a reputation and a character. My reputation is what other people say I am—over this I have no control. Character is what I really am—over this I have all control. This is what concerns me."

Too often we get caught up in building a reputation instead of character. We get overly concerned about what others think of us instead of developing our genuine selves. When our character is solid, our reputation takes care of itself. It is our character that will ultimately dictate our conduct. What can we do to build character?

> We teach what we know; we reproduce what we are.

DENY YOURSELF

We must learn to allow Jesus to rule as Lord of our lives. It means saying "no" to the wrong things and "yes" to the correct things. Character is forged in the cauldron of sacrifice.

54

Jim Whitaker, the first American to reach the summit of Mt. Everest said, "You never conquer a mountain. Mountains can't be conquered; you conquer yourself—your hopes, your fears." If we are able to deny ourselves, we have learned to conquer ourselves.

DECIDE TO PAY THE PRICE

During World War II Winston Churchill promised his countrymen, "Blood, toil and sweat." This adversity built their character. Everyone pays a price. You either "pay now, and play later; or play now and pay later." Character is developed when there is a willingness to pay now.

DELIBERATELY SACRIFICE

Begin now to sacrifice anything that would keep you from developing strong character. Sacrifice a bit of your time to spend it with God. Spending time with God will allow you to get to know Him. His character will rub off on you and mold your character.

A CHARACTER STUDY

Mark 10:46–52 tells the story of Bartimaeus. This story provides us with five principles that will communicate to others who we are. By living out these ideas, we will be leaders who communicate what is most important—how to really live life!

1. Initiate action.

"When Bartimaeus heard that Jesus of Nazareth was nearby, he began to shout . . ." (verse 47). Bartimaeus didn't wait for an invitation. He heard Jesus was coming. He wanted to get His attention, so he raised his voice and called out.

Leaders don't wait to get things done. Instead, they wade into getting things done. Clement Stone encouraged people to awake in the morning and say fifty times, "Do it now, do it now, do it now, do it now . . ." He instructed people to repeat the same phrase fifty more times before going to bed in the evening. Bottom line: Do it now! Initiate action.

2. Determine to move ahead.

"'Be quiet!' many of the people yelled at him" (verse 48). The people around Bartimaeus wanted him to be quiet. They didn't want him to bother Jesus. But he refused to succumb to their discouragement. He cried out louder and more often.

In the 1950s, a clergyman was discouraged about the rejection notices he had received from various publishers. He became so frustrated that he threw his manuscript in the wastebasket. His wife reached to salvage it, but he told her sternly, "We've wasted enough time on it. I forbid you to take it from the wastebasket."

She heeded his words, but took it to one more publisher, still inside the wastebasket. The publisher bought it. The book was *The Power of Positive Thinking.* The young clergyman was Norman Vincent Peale. Mrs. Peale's determination spawned the writing career of her husband.

3. Be enthusiastic about life.

"When Jesus heard him, he stopped and said, 'Tell him to come here.'. . . Bartimaeus threw aside his coat, jumped up, and came to Jesus" (verses 49–50). When the opportunity came to meet Jesus, Bartimaeus went after it. He didn't need to be asked twice. He just needed to know that Jesus had called

> Nothing great was ever achieved without enthusiasm.
> Ralph Waldo Emerson

for him. Approach all of life with an attitude of enthusiasm. People like to be where there is an atmosphere of energy, encouragement, and enthusiasm.

4. Have awareness of direction.

"'What do you want me to do for you?' Jesus asked. 'My rabbi,' the blind man said, 'I want to see'" (verse 51). Bartimaeus knew what he wanted. He wanted to see! If you don't know where you are going, any road will do. When

57

you know where you are going, only the best road will do. Clear direction provides those you lead with confidence.

5. Maintain strength in adversity.

"And Jesus said to him, 'Go, for your faith has healed you'" (verse 52). Bartimaeus lived his faith, and so should we. Life has adversities that cannot be avoided. Learn to encounter them with strength, insight, and a positive attitude.

What we *are* as leaders is more pivotal than what we *say* as leaders. Our language should be an extension of our lifestyles; our conversation an overflow of our character. What we communicate should match our conduct.

KEY POINTS

- Six Tips for Effective Public Speaking: be believable, know your audience, share yourself, prepare well, be enjoyable, and be empowered.
- To develop character you need to initiate action, determine to move ahead, be enthusiastic about life, have awareness of direction, and maintain strength in adversity.

DISCUSSION QUESTIONS

1. Describe your communication style.

2. What is something you need to clearly communicate?

3. What would you like to be remembered for?

4. What character issues might need to be addressed in your life?

ACTION STEPS

1. If you are in a teaching role this week, secure ample time to prepare.

2. Review the "Six Tips for Effective Public Speaking." Where do you need work?

3. List ten people to whom you can write a note of appreciation. Send them each a note.

4. Develop a filing system to keep stories, illustrations, etc.

RESOURCES

- John Maxwell—*Leadership 101*
- James Watkins—*Communicate to Change Lives in Person and Print*
- James Watkins (Ed.)—*Writers on Writing*

4 CULTIVATE RELATIONSHIPS

A leader is someone who brings people together.

George W. Bush

We live in a relational world. Success or failure in life is built on our ability to get along with others. It was Charlie Brown who said, "I love humanity, it's people I can't stand." Many of us approach our leadership from this perspective. We forget that people make the world go around. Our willingness to relate well with them often determines our success in leading them. People skills, relating to others, positive interaction—whatever term you attach to it—is a must for leaders. People tend to follow someone with whom they have a good relationship. We all lead through relationships. Leaders accept the fact that they must deal with people. The leader's ability to navigate relationships will, to a great extent, determine their effectiveness.

CONFLICT IN RELATIONSHIPS

I participated recently in a roundtable discussion about conflict in the church. The consensus tended to lean toward the acceptance of conflict. One individual said that he felt conflict was unavoidable. I disagreed with him. I don't think there has to be conflict in the church, but there does have to be confrontation. When confrontation is avoided by leadership, conflict will occur.

Conflict arises when confrontation is shunned or ignored. Conflict comes between people when issues are left to resolve themselves. Conflict means unresolved problems; confrontation means problems resolved. Conflict is letting things ride; confrontation is bringing in the reins. Conflict is talking about others; confrontation is talking to others. Conflict separates the body of believers; positive confrontation strengthens the body of Christ.

> A mark of leadership is the ability to handle conflict in such a way that it is mutually helpful. This is the beginning of loving confrontation.
>
> — Unknown

Do you see the trend? Conflict comes into organizations when leaders refuse to take responsibility for dealing with people problems. When you work with people, there will be problems. They will disagree, misunderstand, and say

61

things that would be best left unsaid. It is up to the leader to handle relational concerns.

The key is to do all you can to ensure a positive confrontation. Paul tells us, "Do all that you can to live in peace with everyone" (Rom, 12:18). One aspect of doing our part is the willingness to confront those who need to be confronted. Confrontation is not easy, nor is it enjoyable. Leaders, however, who are willing to do the difficult (confront), will discover the enjoyable (healthier relationships).

EIGHT STEPS TO POSITIVE CONFRONTATION
1. Recognize the need for spiritual discernment.

The goal is to have relationships healed, not emotional carnage strewn all around a room. Since our desire is to have God glorified in the life of His people, the best way to see this achieved is to ask God to be central in the conversation. James encourages us to ask God for discernment. "If you need wisdom [if you want to know what God wants you to do] ask our generous God, and he will give it to you. He will not rebuke you for asking" (James 1:5).

2. Talk to the right person.

Unfortunately, many in the church would rather talk to anybody but the one they should. No wonder there are those who believe conflict cannot be avoided. Many relational problems in the church could be resolved if people would talk to—instead of about—the person with whom they had a concern.

In the majority of cases, confrontation needs to be done privately. The only time the confrontation should take place in a "group" setting is when several people are involved.

3. Connect in a timely fashion.

Timing is critical. It is best to confront people as close to the situation as possible, though this is not always feasible. Sometimes it is good to wait several days to give emotions a chance to settle down. Remember, the problem should not be spread around to others prior to the confrontation. People who do this say they are merely looking for support, but most often they want to build allies for what they perceive as an upcoming battle.

Don't Prep for Battle, Prep Create the Battle in your mind

4. Get the situation straight.

There are usually three sides to any situation: my side, your side, and the correct side. When resolving conflicts, dig until you have discovered the correct side of the situation. This is where resolution begins. Ask good questions. Listen.

63

5. Clarify the issue.

Be as specific as you can. Why are you having this confrontation? There were three ladies in my church who needed to have a positive confrontation. They had overlapped each other for use of the church kitchen. Two of the ladies felt the other one had arrived a half-hour too early and the other believed the two had wanted to stay a half-hour too long. There were hurt feelings.

I set up an appointment. This situation could easily have become one group against another. The key was to bring the proper people together at one place, at one time. When we got together I made it clear why we needed the meeting. We were there to find out what happened, how it was handled, and how to handle it better the next time an overlap might occur. It was a very positive meeting.

> I know you thought you heard what I said, but what I said is not what you heard.

6. Observe what they are saying.

People say more than we hear. When listening to those who are being confronted, or who are confronting others, hear them—but also try to see them. What is their perspective on life? What situations or experiences are causing them to act a certain way? Filter the comments that are made. Some

64

people tend to exaggerate; others understate situations. Pray for wisdom to discern what they are really saying.

7. Watch your attitude.
Make sure all feelings are aired before responding. When people believe they have been backed into a corner, they defend themselves. Words might be said that will cause you to respond in anger. Rely on the Spirit and keep your cool. An angry confrontation will always result in conflict.

8. Hold no grudges.
In a healthy organization people should be able to confront one another and have disagreements without harboring grudges or resentments. Recognize the issue. *Confront* it; *deal* with it; *forget* it. If a confrontation does not bring resolution, set up a time to meet again. Make sure those involved have an opportunity to air their feelings.

TWO SIDES OF CRITICISM
There is an old adage that says, "If you can't stand the heat, get out of the kitchen." This describes leadership. If you don't want to be criticized, then you probably won't enjoy leading others. Criticism is a by-product of leadership. As a leader, not only will you be criticized, but you may have to critique those you lead.

Criticism is seen from two perspectives: constructive and destructive. Most people feel that criticism is constructive when they criticize others, but destructive when others criticize them. Leadership demands we learn both ends of the spectrum. We need to be able to handle the criticism thrown our way and we must constructively critique.

THE ART OF BEING CRITICIZED

It was the second of two Christmas Eve services. I was sitting in the front pew, next to my, then, nine-year-old son Scott. He had been through one service and was at the second because he had a part in it. We were singing some of the great Christmas hymns. Scott leaned over and whispered, "Your sermon was boring."

There it was! In four to-the-point words he had critiqued all my hard work. Did it sting? Sure it did. Did he mean it? Sure he did. Was his spirit right? Yes.

It is important to determine the spirit in which criticism is given. Three questions will help in making a fair evaluation:

- How was the criticism given?
- When was it given?
- Why was it given?

A critical remark may be given judgmentally. A judgment is more of a sentencing than an expressed concern. If a person leaves you no benefit of the doubt, their criticism is not meant for your improvement. Listen to it, but don't dwell long.

Filter Criticism

Criticism should always be filtered. Primarily, it should be run through the "who" filter. Who is giving the criticism? Are they typically critical? Is it an individual whose opinion you respect?

I had been on staff for a short time. A certain couple in the church was highly critical of me. They didn't like the ministries I implemented. They weren't fond of the things I did. They were bothered by what I said and how I said it.

They wrote a six-page letter criticizing me. They sent it to my senior pastor. He called me

> 101 Percent Relationship Principle: Find the 1 percent you can agree on and give it 100 percent of your effort.

into his office and shared something that changed my entire perspective on their barrage of negativity.

"Phil, don't take any of this too personally. You are just the newest one on staff." The quizzical look on my face told him I didn't understand. He went on, "This family has been critical of every person on this staff. They were after me when I first arrived. You just happen to be the newest, so it's your turn."

This was the filter I needed to use. They were always after someone. What they were saying was being watered down because of its frequency.

There are others whose criticism really counts, and when they say something negative you must perk up and listen. They may be the people in your area of responsibility who hardly say anything. They are active, growing, and supportive. When they have a concern, they have earned the right to be heard. Run them through the filter of "they have something to say."

> No leader is exempt from criticism, and his humility will nowhere be seen more clearly than in the manner in which he accepts and reacts to it.
>
> J. Oswald Sanders

Check the Crowd

When you receive criticism, check the crowd. Are you hearing something you have heard before? Are you hearing it from several people?

I have always considered myself a people person. I enjoy people—being with them and laughing with them. I was hurt when someone mentioned to me that I didn't really listen to them. This person said that my attention always seemed divided. Honestly, I didn't give this much thought, until I heard it from someone else. I then asked some others if they felt it was a fair criticism. Sadly, but politely, they agreed with it. So I made changes.

Change for the Positive
The key when being criticized is to learn from it. There is a kernel of truth in all criticism. Once that kernel is found, it can be used to start change and improvement.

Here are four questions to ask yourself after being criticized:

- The question of validity: What, if anything, is true about the criticism?
- The question of insight: What can I learn from this criticism?

There is a kernel of truth in all criticism.

- The question of growth: What can I change in order to be a better person?
- The question of action: What will I do as a result of this criticism?

CRITIQUING FOR GROWTH
The legitimate purpose of criticism is to help people do better the next time. I suggest the following principles:

69

Be a Coach

A critic says things to point out the problems. A coach points things out in order to correct them. Tom Landry, the former head coach of the Dallas Cowboys, was the consummate teacher. If players made an error he would pull them from the game. The player would stand next to him and Landry would say, "Do you understand what you did wrong?"

If the player answered yes, Coach Landry would ask him to explain the correct way. If the answer was no, he would explain to him the proper method. The player would then be sent back into the game. This is coaching.

Offer Solutions

Anybody can say something is wrong, but it takes a real leader to find alternatives. The story is told of a conversation Thomas Carlyle had with his mother as he was heading out to a speaking engagement.

"And where might you be going, Thomas?" she asked. "Mother," he replied, "I'm going to tell the people what is wrong with the world."

70

"Aye, Thomas," his mother responded, "but are you going to tell them what to do about it?"

Be Specific

Make sure the person understands exactly what it is you are criticizing. Generalizations usually accomplish nothing. Specifics allow people to know exactly which area needs work.

You might say to someone, "You don't get along with people." This is a criticism, but offers no tangible area to correct. It would be better to say, "You have a blunt way of expressing yourself, which causes you difficulty in your relationships." The specific criticism indicates an area that can be developed.

Be Encouraging

When a criticism is necessary, always leave people with a positive affirmation. Give them an insight into their strengths. Help them see what they do well. Build their confidence by building their self-esteem.

CULTIVATING PEOPLE

Cultivating people—building them up, developing their lives, investing in their future—is a leader's highest priority. We can accomplish this through these three steps: *knowing*, *growing* and *showing*.

Knowing People

You need to get to know those you lead. This is a result of

spending time with them. Spend time finding out who they are. Discover what they do professionally and personally. Remember small things such as their birthdays or anniversaries. Communicate that they are essential to the team.

History records that the explorer Thomas Cook told his crew he would name newly discovered islands after the men who first spotted them. He placed value on his men. They knew they were an integral part of the exploration. He communicated their worth by enlisting them in the discovery of new lands. He valued their observational skills and asked for their input.

Invest your time in developing relationships and building up people. A genuine interest in others can change their life forever. Never underestimate the power generated when people know you care.

Growing People
Here are four suggestions to help you be a leader who will grow others:

Be a Reach-Out Leader. Follow Christ's pattern of servant-leadership. Notice the need before you and make it your personal responsibility to meet that need with the resources available to you.

72

Be a Reliable Leader. Do what you say you will do. Be where you say you will be. Fulfill the promises you make. The people you lead need to be able to depend on you. Be that kind of person!

On a missions trip to Hungary, our group found itself looking for a place to eat in Budapest. None of us knew what Hungarians ate, but we thought, "When in Hungary, do as the Hungarians do." And that is exactly what we did; we ate at one of their most popular places—McDonald's!

Later, we discussed the situation in reverse. Hungarians in search of food in America would see a McDonald's and would welcome it as a familiar sight. They would discover—as we had—that it tasted "just like home."

The McDonald's corporation has discovered the power of consistency. As leaders we would do well to model this example. Be a leader that is reliable and trustworthy. Be dependable in your attitude and actions. When your people know they can count on you, you'll be able to count on them.

Be a Reassuring Leader. When the tough times come, you must be the one to climb over the obstacles and keep on going. When your plans fail, you must be the one to be ready with another plan. When you face difficult situations,

73

it is by your smile of reassurance—your attitude of control—that your people will find the confidence to continue.

On my first trip overseas, I was flying with a friend from Manila to Sebu in the Philippines. My traveling companion was an experienced traveler. The trip down the length of Luzon was a bumpy one due to thunder activity. Halfway through the flight, the plane dropped. The drop was so pronounced that the overhead compartments flew open with a bang! There was a collective passenger gasp. Panic-stricken, I looked over at Paul, who was reading, apparently untroubled by the turbulence.

"Is this normal?" I asked uneasily.

He raised his head, looked me straight in the eye and replied calmly, "It is very normal when flying through large thunderheads." With that, he returned to his book.

That was reassurance. His demeanor, attitude, and experience put him in position to instill confidence. His reassurance was exactly what I needed to put my fears behind me.

Be a Resourceful Leader. Give those you lead whatever is necessary to get the job done. Provide them with training, tools, ideas and time, and put them in touch with others who have the expertise they need. Challenge them, equip them, and watch them reproduce themselves in others.

Showing People

Be an example. Show them what Christianity is all about! Jesus modeled servant-leadership before He challenged His disciples to be servants. Jesus went to the cross to show us what it means to love.

What do you want your people to do? Are you doing it? Or are you merely asking them to do it? The finest teaching happens when word and deed go hand in hand.

Relationships are the foundation of leadership. You can impact people from a distance, but you will only influence them up close. Relationships put you up close.

KEY POINTS

- Eight Steps to Positive Confrontation: Recognize the need for spiritual discernment. Talk to the right people. Connect in a timely fashion. Get the situation straight. Clarify the issue. Observe what they are saying. Watch your attitude. Hold no grudges.
- Questions to Help Evaluate Criticism: What is true? What can I learn? What can I change? What will I do?

DISCUSSION QUESTIONS

1. What issues do you find yourself confronting?

2. How do you relate to difficult people?

3. What might you change to better relate to them?

4. How do you handle criticism?

5. Who are you currently cultivating?

ACTION STEPS

1. Employ these questions with a conflict you are currently facing:

In your opinion, what is the problem?

What do you believe needs to be done?

What is the best possible solution?

What are you willing to do to resolve the issue?

2. Schedule a meeting with all of the people involved with the conflict.

3. Choose someone new this week to begin cultivating a relationship with.

RESOURCES

- Alan Loy McGinnis—*Bringing out the Best in People*
- John Maxwell—*Winning with People Person*
- Wayne Schmidt—*Power Plays*

5 MODEL SPIRITUAL EXCELLENCE

*We cannot lead anyone else further
than we have been ourselves.*

John Maxwell

What we do will always flow out of who we are. Neglecting the inner life will eventually result in some form of bankruptcy; we can only withdraw based on that which we have deposited.

The ATM is a marvelous invention of convenience. You need cash? Stop by your ATM and get it. The bank doesn't have to be open. The tellers don't have to be available. All you need is your ATM card and your PIN and the cash is at your fingertips—or is it?

It would be nice if it always worked that way, but without regular deposits you will soon encounter the reality of insufficient funds. The amount of your withdrawal is dependent on the amount of your deposit.

Leaders are constantly withdrawing from their personal reserve. When they give of themselves by serving others, they are making withdrawals. Unless they make regular deposits, leaders cannot continue to make withdrawals without becoming emotionally and spiritually bankrupt.

Bankruptcy occurs when the indications of insufficient funds are ignored. Here are some indicators of an account near depletion: prayerlessness, lower energy, less time in the Word, a sense of gloom, unhealthy attraction to the opposite sex, and the inability or the lack of desire to deal with personal temptation.

CROSS VERSUS CREDITS

It is through the regular and consistent development of a relationship with God that leadership is enhanced. Neglecting spiritual growth will stunt our leadership. Leaders tend to focus on *doing* things. We plan events, strategize, make and keep appointments, and prepare lessons. None of this is wrong—unless the leader is not taking time to make the necessary spiritual deposits. Leaders need to develop spiritual depth. We need to design systems for making regular deposits.

The story is told of a fish company on the east coast that prided itself on providing the freshest fish to its customers. If the fish wasn't fresh, it wasn't sent. This task was not too difficult when sending the stock locally. However, as the company expanded, a new problem came to light: how to keep the fish fresh when transporting it over great distances.

The most logical method seemed to be to ship the fish in salt water. But even though it was the fish's natural habitat, the salt water idea did not bring about the desired results. It was hoped that freezing the fish while still fresh would lock in the fresh taste. But thawed freshness is not truly fresh. Taste does not lie.

Then a new idea surfaced. It seemed completely illogical. In fact, everyone thought it was a joke. But this company was desperate, and desperation breeds strange bedfellows. So the idea was put to the test.

To everyone's amazement, it worked! The fish were arriving fresh! They tasted as if they had just been scooped from their natural habitat.

What was this innovative and creative idea? The fish company placed the species' natural enemy inside every tank. With their enemy nearby, the fish had to stay alert and keep moving. This kept them strong and fresh.

If we are to stay fresh, vibrant, alive, and strong as leaders, we need to be aware of our enemies. One critical area of attack is the tendency to look for love and acceptance from sources other than God. We are caught up in the battle of "the Cross vs. Credits."

The Cross is the source of our salvation and adoption into God's family. God's love and acceptance are ours because of the Cross—not because we have done anything to earn them. The Cross is our only true source of power.

Instead of focusing on Christ's work at Calvary, we begin to pay attention to our credits—these accomplishments become our source of love, acceptance, and power. Our lives become based on what *we* have done, not what *Christ* has done.

We can see the same battle being fought in Galatians 3:1–5. These early Christians began listening to other voices that shouted: "It is Christ *plus* works! Christ *plus* circumcision! Christ *plus* ritual! Christ *plus* the law! Christ's sacrifice is not sufficient, it must be augmented by something we do."

We fall into this same trap. Instead of resting on the Cross and the sufficiency it provides, we rely on our credits. It is the Cross—*plus* our administrative skills. It is the Cross—

plus our teaching and preaching of God's Word. It is the Cross—*plus* our attitude and ability to motivate people.

We need to hone our leadership skills, but they must never become the basis for our love and acceptance before God. We must not live in the arena of accomplishment. The more we accomplish, the greater our accolades, the more our abilities are recognized, the more we need to rely on God.

We need to hear and answer the question Paul submitted to the believers in Galatia. "You were running the race so well. Who has held you back from following the truth?" (Gal. 5:7). Paul is saying to them, and to us, "Who told you your source of power was in anything except the Cross of Jesus Christ?"

Paul had already personally settled the issue of "the Cross vs. Credits" (Phil. 3:1–7). He had been religiously successful. He was a motivated, goal-oriented, make-things-happen man. This was not where his acceptance and love originated though. His source, his center, his frame of reference was grounded in the Cross of Jesus Christ.

82 Let's resist the temptation to focus on what we do at the expense of who we are. When Christ is our focus and the Cross is our source, we become free. We no longer agonize

over being good enough; we are free to allow God to work through us. We can spend our time investing in the lives of people—not because it boosts our egos or increases our worth in the eyes of God—but because God cared so much for us that we desire to care for others.

It is a daily battle to keep the Cross central. In Galatians six, Paul provides four practical methods:

1. Pour into others (verses 1–2).
When we take our eyes off the Cross we become concerned with our own needs. We must pour into the lives of others. Ministering to their needs keeps us dependent on God and prevents us from becoming self-centered and ingrown.

2. Proper self-perception (verses 3–5).
Avoid getting caught up in "other" comparison. We can always find someone less effective and use that comparison to inflate our ego; or we can look at someone who is more gifted and become unnecessarily discouraged. We need to test our own actions. We are responsible only for those gifts and talents God has given us.

> When Christ is our focus and the cross is our source, we become free.

When we compare ourselves to those who seem less successful, we tend to glory in our own strength. Our success becomes our own source of pride. When that happens, the Cross slips out of its central location. Our worth moves from the Cross to our own accomplishments.

When comparing ourselves to those who are more successful, we tend to become discouraged. We forget that God created us the way we are, with a unique and special purpose in life. We focus on what we cannot do, instead of what we can do because of the Cross.

3. Plant seeds in the proper soil (verses 6–8).

Paul is reminding us to be careful where we sow our seed. If we put our hope and trust in our own strengths and accomplishments, we will surely reap a harvest of disillusionment and failure. But if we plant our faith in the Cross of Christ, our lives will abound with joy and our influence will be far-reaching.

It takes only a few months to grow a squash, but many years to grow an oak tree. The question we must ask of our leadership is this: Are we looking for immediate, temporary results, or are we willing to work toward a permanent and final outcome?

4. Persevere in the difficult times (verses 9–10).

Perseverance is the ability to continue, even when results are not evident. It is doing right even though it is not convenient. Perseverance is what it takes to win.

Many have heard the story of Winston Churchill who, several years after World War II, was asked to be the keynote speaker at a preparatory school. It had been quite a while since he had given a speech of any kind. Age had robbed him of much of his strength and agility, so his movement to the podium was painfully slow.

He stood, pausing a few moments to take stock of the young audience. His eyes still held the fire of the man who led England through one of her darkest hours. All attention was focused on this great man. What words of wisdom, what stirring oratory, what passion would he convey to the young people gathered on this momentous occasion? With a strong voice Mr. Churchill spoke. "Never give up! Never give up! Never give up!" And, with that, he turned and made his way back to his seat.

Never give up! Persevere! Move steadily ahead! Perseverance is what it takes to keep Christ central in your life. Perseverance is the necessary ingredient when putting the Cross over credits. When you feel the most like quitting, don't!

DISCIPLINES THAT MATTER

Discipline is a choice. It is not dictated by feelings or circumstances. Discipline is a means to an end; it is the vehicle through which desire is realized. Discipline enables us to accomplish goals and fulfill dreams. It is through disciplined living that we grow spiritually.

The natural flow of life is downward. It is a universal law that life moves toward chaos and decay. If you don't spend time cultivating your garden, weeds accumulate and flowers die. If you don't take care of your house, the paint peels, windows stick, and wood rots. Neglecting your spiritual life will bring the same result.

> God intends the Disciplines of the spiritual life to be for ordinary human beings: People who have jobs, who care for children, who must wash dishes and mow lawns.
>
> Richard Foster

Critical in making regular deposits into our spiritual ATM is connecting with God. We need to determine those things that help us connect to God. Identifying those, we need to do them consistently. I will suggest four here. This is not exhaustive, but it will give you a start.

Prayer

Prayer is hard work—it does not come naturally. We must spend consistent time in prayer. It makes no difference when and where—the important thing is that we pray.

Pray for those you lead and for the salvation of people you know. Pray for wisdom and courage and compassion and love. Ask God to reveal himself to you and use your life for His glory.

In 2 Chronicles 20, Jehoshaphat finds himself in a difficult situation. Three nations—the Moabites, the Ammonites and some of the Meunites—have come to make war with him. What does he do? He prays. He knows that only God's intervention will get him out of this situation. He models three truths we would be well to remember when we pray.

Be reminded of who God is. ". . . You are ruler of all the kingdoms of the earth. You are powerful and mighty; no one can stand against you!" (verse 6).

Be reminded of the God you serve. He is strong and capable; He is in command and will never fail you.

Be reminded of what God has done in the past. "O our God, did you not drive out those who lived in this land when your people Israel arrived?" (verse 7).

Remembering gave him strength for the trial ahead. Remembering the past can provide resources for the present.

Ask God to do it again. "O our God, won't you stop them?" (verse 12).

Jehoshaphat is saying, "Do it again, Lord. Take care of this enemy. Give us victory." When you pray, ask God to do what He does best—work through His people to bring glory to His name.

Worship

Worship is the celebration of God in daily life. Praising God through songs and hymns is a pathway to worship. Through praise our attention is focused on the one we serve. Through praise our souls are lifted and our worship is made complete.

> If worship is a transforming experience, then it must result in service that transforms the world.
>
> Warren Wiersbe

Worship is practiced corporately (Heb. 10:25). God's people need to come together to be encouraged, instructed, and to lift praise to God. It is through this corporate praise that we are built up and strengthened to be the church of Jesus Christ to the world.

88

Worship is practiced in the ordinary moments of life. Elijah encountered God in the "sound of a gentle whisper" (1 Kings 19:12). We miss God when we look for Him only in the big events of life. He is in the wonder of a cleansing rain. He is in the mundane process of house cleaning. He fills the quietness of midnight. God is in the everyday, the ordinary, the common moments that make up our lives.

Corporate praise and practicing the presence of God in the ordinary will enhance your worship. The discipline of worship will increase your effectiveness as a leader.

Witness

Witnessing is sharing who you know—Jesus—with whom you know—friends, relatives, associates and neighbors. The definition is not as important as the action. God has called us all to be witnesses (Acts 1:8). He wants to use us to spread the good news of Jesus Christ to those around us. As others hear and accept the gospel, His kingdom grows and flourishes.

We need to pray for open doors and open hearts. We should pray for clarity of proclamation. We must pray that we will be able to explain the gospel in such a way that people will understand.

We need to develop relationships of integrity. People see our lives before they ever hear our words. We must be people of integrity, honesty, and authenticity. We must let God's light shine through our lives, even when times are tough.

We must discern opportunities. We cannot afford to turn our backs on any chance we get to witness to the love of God, either by what we say or what we do.

Exposure to the Word

God's Word is our instruction book. It's full of principles that have life-changing power. When we consistently allow the Word of God to wash over us, something happens. We are altered in our thoughts, actions, and insights. Reading is one method of being exposed to the Scripture, but there are others as well.

We can hear God's Word through sermons, CDs, DVDs, and Podcasts to name a few of many methods. The proclamation of God's Word is central to our growth as a believer. Develop methods to help retain what you hear.

We study God's Word. When we study, we search for facts, principles, key themes, main points, etc. You may choose to incorporate commentaries, Bible dictionaries, and other study helps, but if you are unable to do so, don't be discouraged from digging deeper.

We can memorize God's Word. The human brain retains everything, but not everything can be recalled. Memorization is a way of making sure scriptural truths can be recalled when they are needed. Memorization techniques vary from person to person. Find what works for you and put it into practice.

We can meditate on God's Word. This is the process of thinking about God's Word during the day and applying it to life. Look for situations, attitudes, actions and circumstances where God's Word can be applied. Meditation is a method of using Scripture to cleanse your mind.

Developing as a leader takes discipline. Discipline is necessary because the natural flow of life is toward chaos and decay. Through proper discipline, we stem the flow and make our way against the tide.

YES, THERE IS A HOLY SPIRIT

We are told to "be filled with the Holy Spirit" (Eph. 5:18). It is this filling that becomes our source for growth. When we accept God the Son into our lives, He immediately restores our relationship with God the Father and He implants in us God the Spirit.

Picture two glasses of equal size. They have the capacity to hold the same amount of liquid. Both glasses are filled to the brim with water. However, there is one difference: one of the glasses has a pile of marbles at the bottom. Are the glasses filled to the same level with water? The answer is yes. They both are filled to the brim. Do both glasses have the same amount of water in them? The answer is no. Why? Because in one glass, marbles are taking up the space liquid could.

We are like those glasses. Even though the Spirit lives in us, we may not be experiencing the fullness that could be ours. Perhaps it is an attitude, a habit, an unresolved conflict, or a negative thought life that is keeping us from all that God has for us. We must identify these "marbles" and, with the help of the Holy Spirit, remove them from our lives. Only then can we be *filled* with the Spirit and begin to grow.

> Every man is as full of the Spirit as he wants to be. Make your heart a vacuum and the spirit will rush in.
>
> A.W. Tozer

WHAT IS THIS FILLING?
It is to be cleansed (1 John 1:9).

The Holy Spirit cleanses us from all impurities. The Spirit is the refining fire in our lives. As the Holy Spirit rushes in, impurities are pushed out. The Spirit flushes our spiritual systems.

It is to be crucified with Christ (Gal. 2:20).

It is through the death of the things that entangle us that we discover the freedom to be the holy people God has called us to be. It is a trade off. We are crucified with Christ so that it is He who lives in us. He is the controlling agent. The Spirit handles our steering mechanism.

It is to be a container for His power (Acts 1:8).

The power we contain determines our ability to share the gospel message with boldness. When we contain His power, we cannot be contained. The Spirit is the fuel for our drive.

The key to being full of the Spirit is "marble" removal. Allow the Spirit into your life on a daily basis. Ask that any "stuff" that is at the bottom of your glass be removed. Losing your marbles may be the best thing you can do for your spiritual growth. Be a leader who has lost their marbles.

COMMITMENT TO SPIRITUAL EXCELLENCE

Being committed allows us to move ahead in the face of all odds. Once we have committed ourselves to grow, there is little that can hold us back. Commitment is where the struggle ends. I want to encourage you to make four personal commitments.

1. Commit to ability (Col. 3:23–24).

God has given you ability; commit yourself to putting it to work. Too often, people concentrate on what they are not able to do, instead of cultivating their abilities.

A friend of mine was born with his left hand underdeveloped. He competes in sports, runs two businesses, and is actively involved in a church plant. He could have approached life bemoaning his lack of two hands. Instead, he has chosen to look at what he can do. He is committed to the ability he has. Leader, this is what your attitude should be. Be committed to your ability. God has given it to you; He expects you to use it.

2. Commit to achievement (Phil. 3:13–14).

A leader who is committed to achievement will be focused on potential, not problems. Polio was a world-wide problem until Dr. Jonas Salk took it on as a project and determined to find the solution. Press on toward the end, moving ahead to achieve that to which God has called you.

3. Commit to authenticity (Phil. 2:5).

Our authenticity lies in being honest and open with others. Follow Christ's example of love, compassion, and servant-leadership. He did not pretend to be anyone but himself. He poured himself into the lives of the people around Him and changed their lives forever.

94

Authenticity is making right choices more often than wrong. It is giving people your best shot. It is sticking to your convictions in the midst of a deceitful world. By doing this you will be a person who will make a difference!

4. Commit to application (Phil. 4:9).

What you learn does no good unless it is applied. Spend time in Bible study and prayer. Then resolve to use the truths of Scripture to change your attitudes and actions. God can do great things through leaders who are willing to put to use what they have been taught.

Commitment is the key to consistent growth. Without commitment, you will be easily deterred from the goals you have set. Be resolved. Make the choice! Commit yourself to *ability*, *achievement*, *authenticity*, and *application*.

KEY POINTS
- Pour into others. Have proper self-perception. Plant seeds in the proper soil. Persevere in the difficult times.
- Be cleansed. Be crucified. Be contained.

DISCUSSION QUESTIONS

1. What enhances your prayer life?

2. What do you enjoy most about corporate worship?

3. What do you do to feed on the word of God?

4. What are the abilities that God has given you?

5. What keeps people from being authentic with each other?

ACTION STEPS

1. List three of your strengths. List three of your weaknesses. Where do you tend to dwell? What might you do to fully recognize God's sufficiency in your life?

2. To remove the marbles in your life: Identify potential or existing shortcomings in your life. Admit they need to be dealt with. Find scriptures that address your shortcomings. Become accountable to someone else.

RESOURCES

- Richard Foster—*Celebration of Discipline*
- Dallas Willard—*Spirit of the Disciplines*
- Keith Drury—*With Unveiled Faces*